Waiting For The Ice Cream Man:
How I Found True Love Through The Power of A Simple Prayer

By Simisola Okai

What Others Have Said

"This book is one person's honest and vulnerable take on what abstinence meant for her and her marriage. A refreshing read that runs counter to our sex-saturated culture."

- Megan Alexander, Author, "Faith In The Spotlight"

"Reading Simi's account reminded me again of a piece my old music teacher wrote for her majesty Queen Elizabeth in the 90's "forever truth is better than falsehood......Veritas!" the effortless manner Simi takes us through some very personal and painful episodes is truly empowering. We all hurt as we all wait but can be encouraged that God hears and answers."

- Muyiwa Olarewaju, Broadcaster & Recording Artist

"In a society that is skeptical about God-ordained relationships, this book is a beautiful testament to the benefits of waiting & trusting God for a life partner."

-Abimbola Komolafe, Senior Pastor, RCCG Jubilee Church, Manchester UK

Waiting for The Ice Cream Man

All Scripture quotations, unless otherwise indicated, are taken

from The Holy Bible, King James Version. Cambridge Edition:

1769; King James Bible Online, 2017.

www.kingjamesbibleonline.org.

Cover design : Richard Klein

Interior design: Devyn Maher

Cover photo : © Tejumola Komolafe 2017

Published by:
NyreePress Literary Group
Fort Worth, TX 76161
1-800-972-3864
www.nyreepress.com

ISBN print: 978-1-956305-81-1

Library of Congress Control Number: pending
Categories: Non Fiction / Relationships / Christian Living
Printed in the United States of America

Dedication

This book is dedicated to my first and forever love, Jesus Christ, and of course to my Ice Cream Man, Sam Okai. Doing life with you and our children makes every day so incredibly sweet.

Contents

Forward

"All the single ladies, (all the single ladies) Now put your hands up. Oh, oh, oh…" (Beyoncé)

"I have seen the burden God has laid on the human race. He has made everything beautiful in its time" (Ecclesiastes 3:10-11a).

This is a journey of "boyfriendlessness." It's a journey of singleness. It's a journey of painful waiting which ended up in an inspired life of joy! Everyone desires to be loved and wanted. Everyone has longed for someone to love at one time or another.

If you have ever pursued the need to be loved, if you have ever been curious about the effects of needing to be loved can have on singles, if you have ever prayed and prayed and prayed for Mr. or Mrs. Right to come, or if you have ever wondered if the wait is worth it, then Simisola Okai's compelling story of singleness will appeal to you. Written with warmth and openness, every page is crammed full of hints so you can laugh and gain from them.

The fact that I know Simisola Okai personally, indeed, the fact that I know her "Ice-cream fleece" story makes reading it come close to home. Simisola Okai is my niece. Many years ago, when I visited my brother and his family in Jos, back in Nigeria, I was lodged in her room. I remember praying fervently in that room, being led by the Holy Spirit to 'break' some things. It was a spiritual warfare type of prayer, having perceived something contrary hanging over her life. I asked that God would take over her life, protect, and use her mightily for His glory.

I'm not surprised to see what God has done and what He's doing through Simisola. There are many things that have caught my attention about this princess niece of mine: her love for journaling, her command of the English language—both oral and written—her princessly demeanor, her love for kids, her faith, and most importantly her passion for God and His kingdom. *Waiting For The Ice Cream Man: How I Found True Love Through The Power Of A Simple Prayer* is Simisola Okai's personal journey, from being "a boy-crazy" girl to a prayer-lover, Jesus-chasing girl. It is a story you won't want to put down until you get to the last page. "In those times," according to Simisola, "I went through the excruciating pain of rejection, where I was forced to grapple with the onslaught of emotion and doubt it brought to my heart."

Whether you have formed a habit of looking down on yourself or you are overwhelmed with a lack of self-esteem, this book will put the wind in your sail. It will encourage you to keep on going and not give up. Although the journey you are on looks like it's taking forever and you are even beginning to lose hope, there are so many intriguing stories within the pages of this book that will give you goosebumps—including the dream, the ice-cream episode, and the letters of faith to her future husband.

Simisola Okai's personal experience, her "prise de conscience" of who she is in Christ, as well as her encounter with Him will open your eyes to the fact that God is "in the business of matchmaking and He is the author of romance." In the end, you will realize that your painful wait is divinely orchestrated, and it is working for your own good.

In conclusion, Simisola Okai's *Waiting for the Ice Cream Man* is a journey of "waiting"—waiting in pain, waiting in faith on God, waiting in style, and making the best of the wait.

Enjoy!

Yinka Opadiya (PhD French, Innsbruck Austria.)
Co-Pastor, Every Nation Christian Church
Sydney Australia.

Prologue:
Worth the Wait

I believe there are a million other people like me who have struggled with one of the most painful, yet necessary, elements to life: waiting. I must write this story, my story, just as it is. I cannot help but feel that God wants to create something beautiful out of the pain I have experienced through waiting; more specifically, my journey of waiting for my husband. God works all things together for good, and I know that my case is no different.

Through my journey, I came to the realization that the wait was not about getting; it was not about obtaining the ultimate prize of a husband. The wait had a purpose; the wait was part of the process. It was part of the work God was doing in me. He allowed it to continue so I could learn, through personal experience, something beautiful about His character. It was painful for me to wait, and to hope, for something I had no evidence would come to pass. During my single years, I asked myself, "Who will I be if not a wife and a mother?" I was scared to find out, scared to imagine a life without my husband by my side.

Looking back, I think God wanted to show me that I didn't have to have those things in my life to be complete. I had to learn to be at peace and be content with the woman I was becoming, without the approval of another man. God's approval was the only opinion that truly mattered.

There were times when I wondered if my expectation for a marriage relationship was too great. So many people have desired and attempted marriage with little success. What made me think my story would be any different? I suppose that was the reason I had been cautious about who I gave my heart to. I knew that it was impossible for me to choose the right partner on my own, so I had to learn to lean on God and His direction for my life completely. I was so vulnerable, yet I only wanted to be vulnerable to my loving Father in heaven.

Throughout my journey, there were times when I opened my heart to developing a friendship with certain godly men, hoping it would turn into something more, but it never did. In all those occasions, the guys I was interested in did not feel the same way about me. In those times, I went through the excruciating pain of rejection, where I was forced to grapple with the onslaught of emotion and doubt it brought to my heart. It was hard not to take it personally, hard not to feel ugly, unattractive, and unwanted. I asked God, "If I am so pretty, how come none of the guys I am interested in see that?"

God would tell me, "*I don't want you to build your self-esteem around man, because he will disappoint you. I want you to see yourself as I see you. I want you to know how much I esteem you, how I find you so beautiful, so endearing, so incredible. Find your self-worth in My words. Find your confidence in Me, and it will never be taken away from you.*"

Throughout my teens and through to my late twenties, leaning on God and waiting for Him to choose my husband brought no visible fruit. In a way, that was the hardest part because there were times I wondered if I was doing something wrong: asking the wrong questions, behaving the wrong way. I suffered from an over-eating disorder and wondered many times if my weight issues kept me from God's blessings. I would think to myself, *maybe if I were more obedient in eating the right foods and losing the right amount of weight, my husband would find me.* I wondered, because I knew I couldn't be mad at God for my state of "boyfriendlessness," God would only give me the best, and I knew His character was to never withhold anything that was good from me. Through all of my questioning, I realized one thing—even if the problem was with me, even if my weight had been a hindering factor, God told me that His power was made perfect in my weakness. My weaknesses have never hindered God from moving miraculously in my life. In fact, it was in my weakest moments that I have seen God move in unfathomable ways. It was in the times when things have seemed the most impossible that God had shown Himself strong and made a way out of no way. In the end, I realized that I could not blame God for my state of singleness, nor should I blame myself. The only other conclusion it left me with was this: the *waiting* was not an accident or an unfortunate event. It had purpose. It was God's will for me; therefore, it was a good thing.

The simple truth was, I was scared of confronting the underlying issues of my life. I wanted to tell myself that having a husband would help me escape the fears I had about being alone. I was afraid of what it was God was trying to do through me as a single woman. Inside my heart, I knew that the work God was doing through this wait was for my own good. He was building a foundation in me. He was centering my source of strength to know that, no matter where I was or who I was with, He would always be my Rock. Somehow, I knew God wanted me to remember this time when I had no one else to hold on to, no one else's arm to lean on but His own.

My prayer is that my journey will help you to believe that God is still in the business of matchmaking. In fact, He is the author of romance, and He will help you write your love story, if you will only give Him the pen.

Chapter 1
A Dress Like Cinderella

"Many waters cannot quench love,
neither can the floods drown it."
~Song of Solomon 8:7

I don't know what it was about Cinderella, but as a young girl, I imagined my story would unfold just like hers. She began in unfortunate circumstances, but by the end, everything turned around for her, and she found a perfect prince who brought her fame, love, and fortune. In my mind, all I had to do was meet my prince and everything in my life would magically fall into place.

I was an impressionable young girl who bought into the Cinderella dream. One day my prince would come, pick me up on his stallion, and we would ride off into the sunset together. I also imagined living in a castle complete with a butler, maidservants, and a live-in-nanny. I would, of course, have flawless hair, perfectly manicured nails, and a beautiful sparkly ball gown to match.

The only problem with my little fantasy was, I didn't have a ball to go to and Prince Charming was nowhere in sight. I looked for him, but to no avail. All I heard was, well...crickets. My Cinderella-life with my Cinderella-dress and Cinderella-castle only existed in my imagination. In my real life, I struggled with my weight, self-esteem, and self-worth. It felt good to fantasize about something that was so far from reality. In my own heart, I didn't feel anywhere close to being worthy of the love of a prince. I pictured Cinderella as a confident, pretty, *skinny* girl, and I was far from that. I had pimples growing out of my face that were the size of Texas. I was overweight and gaining pounds by the week because of my binge-eating disorder. The worse I felt about myself, the more I ate. It was a vicious cycle that I desperately wanted out of, and the only way I felt relief was to imagine a life I didn't have.

Every day, I would struggle with how dark my skin was and resent how tall I was compared to my classmates. I desperately wanted to be the ideal of what I saw on TV screens, because my own reality was too hard for me to face. There were 550 thousand reasons, in my mind, why I felt every other girl was prettier than me. I was never the girl that every boy was asking out, so it felt so much easier to dream about an imaginary prince than to face the reality that it was close to impossible to grab the attention of a real one.

I wanted so badly to grab the attention of a cute boy, probably for all the wrong reasons. My hope was to be seen as the only girl in the room, so special that a guy would do everything in his power to get to me. My directive for how that would happen came from watching re-runs of the television show, *Saved By The Bell.* Back then, it was so important to be "asked out" by a cute guy, or a boyfriend, or a special friend, so it was all I wanted and all I dreamed about.

I remember the anticipation of high school dances where I hoped that love would find me. The dances would come and go, and I wouldn't get a phone call, or even a hallway conversation. I was convinced something was wrong with me. I didn't look like the popular cheerleaders, with their long hair and pretty blue eyes. Even then, I wanted the life I'd read about in high school romance books like *Sweet Valley High*. I wanted the "boyfriend" to call my own. The one that waited for me by my locker, held my hand in the hallways, and saved me a seat during lunch time. I wanted, most of all, to feel special, and I thought only a guy would do that for me.

My romantic run-in with Prince Charming didn't happen during the school week, so I held on to the hope that it was bound to happen at a high school dance. I loved the dance atmosphere. I figured, when I got to the party, the music would stop, the spot light would fall directly unto me, and the guy of my dreams would zone in on me (in my Cinderella dress complete with the glass slippers of course). He would part the crowd, walking towards me as though I was the only girl in the room and whisper in my ear, "Hey Baby, I have been staring at you all night, may I have this dance?"

He would whisk me off onto the dance floor, and we would be swallowed in the vortex of love and romance. That was my fantasy. The reality was that I would go to the dances and pretend like I was having a great time until, without fail, a slow song would come on and people would couple up to slow jams from *Boyz to Men* with their arms wrapped tightly around each other—reminding me yet again that I had no one to call my own.

Those moments are forever etched in my memory because those were the moments I felt most alone. Even though it wasn't true, I was convinced everyone had that special somebody and I was, well... on the lifetime wheel of singleness. I felt unloved, and I certainly didn't feel special or attractive enough for that special somebody. I would walk away from the dance floor pretending I was okay, but inside, my heart was breaking. I wanted love so desperately, but I didn't know how to find it. I wanted that one guy to see me as the only girl in the room even if there were hundreds of other people there; I wanted to be the one he couldn't take his eyes off.

As desperately as I wanted that dream, as I got older, I began to realize life doesn't quite follow such a trajectory. Truth be told, it was my love for reading romance novels and watching romantic movies that had my imagination running so wild. I wanted that life, because somewhere in my mind, I believed that falling in love would solve all my problems; true love conquered all, true love made everything better. The logical side of me knew it was all movie magic that made for the perfect love story. Million-dollar budgets, excellent script writers, and good-looking actors—who were made to look even more perfect with the help of movie makeup and an award-winning film crew—made for the perfect love story. In my own life, there was no violin or orchestra playing in perfect pitch. There was no flawless lighting. There was no scriptwriter—*or so I thought*—writing the perfect story. There was only me, a tall black girl who was convinced she wasn't loveable.

Chapter 2
My First Love

"I am my beloved's and my beloved is mine."
~Song of Solomon 6:3

Eighteen was my number. In my mind, by eighteen I would be dating someone special, and I would let him know that I was ready to take our relationship to the next level. Eighteen seemed like the perfect age, because that was what I was told in my sex education class. I figured that by that time,

I would be a young woman who was madly in love and ready to give my body and soul to my super-hot boyfriend who was also smitten with me. Perfect, right? The litmus test for me to cross the virginity line hinged upon the magic number eighteen. I was ready and eager to fall in love, give my heart away, and begin my dream of happily ever after.

During my early teens, I fell into the haze of boy band mania. It was so bad, that if you looked up the phrase "boy band crazy" in the urban dictionary, you would see a picture of me. Back in the late 90's I was *that girl* with a room full of posters, cd's, and magazines of my favorite boy band members. I was an MTV watching, Total Request Live screaming, super fan. I was everything you would imagine a boy-crazed, teeny bopper would be — and worse.

My band of choice was 'N Sync because I was obsessed with Justin Timberlake; so much so, I wrote in my high school yearbook that my life ambition was to meet him. In the summer of 2000, 'N Sync was on their *No Strings Attached* tour, and to my absolute horror, they weren't coming anywhere near my city. But, I noticed they would be in the Boston area, and that Harvard just so happened to have a summer school program in the same area. I jumped at the opportunity to go and was accepted into Harvard's summer school program, making it to Massachusetts just in time for the concert.

I was pleased with how my summer was going and how everything worked out for me to see 'N Sync. One day, I needed to study so I went to one of the common rooms on the Harvard campus to catch up on some reading. I noticed the TV was on. I looked at the screen and realized it was "In Touch" with Charles Stanley, and thought to myself, *Oh great, another preaching program!* I had grown up in a Christian home and always believed God existed, but He always seemed so far away to me. God was up there somewhere doing His thing, and I was down here doing mine; and I was fine with that.

Listening to Charles Stanley that day was probably the first time I really understood what John 3:16 meant. *"For God so loved the world, that he gave his only begotten Son, that whosoever believeth in him should not perish, but have everlasting life."* (John 3:16, KJV). I'd heard that verse so many times before in Sunday School, but for some reason it hit me that day that all I had to do was believe. I remember sitting through the whole presentation, and at the very end of the program, he gave an invitation to pray the prayer of salvation out loud; so I did. Little did I know the impact that one prayer would have on my entire life. That day, a seed was planted in my heart that would germinate a few years later in a way I never would have expected.

It would be way more dramatic if I told you that I immediately became a kind of super-Christian teenager, but that's not what happened. I had Jesus in my heart, but I lived my life however I pleased; I was still consumed by a desire to fall in love with a boy who had dance moves like Justin Timberlake and a soulful voice to match. Two summers later, just a few months before my eighteenth birthday, love did find me. Yet this love looked like nothing I had read about in the story books. This love was all encompassing and life transforming. It was a love that swept me completely off my feet.

This love encounter happened when I moved to Beaverton, Oregon during the summer of 2002. I had the intention of spending just a few weeks, but one summer turned into a year and a year turned into four. I was still the same boy crazy, hopeless romantic teenager who hoped my love life would model that of Kate Beckinsale's from the movie *Serendipity*. I had just completed my freshman year in college and my quest to find love in the dormitories of my college campus had failed miserably.

In fact, just weeks before moving to Oregon, I was dancing at a club on a bar table with a few of my girlfriends. We frequented nightclubs at least twice a week. I am not sure why I imagined I would find the "one" amongst a throng of half-drunk men looking for a good time. I suppose I was just following the crowd, doing what everybody else was doing. I was hoping to hit the jackpot on love, but I would usually end up bankrupt as I encountered men who had no interest in my intellect or my heart. All they wanted was what I could offer them on a physical level, and for some reason, I had no interest in giving that up. I was still a virgin at the time, not because of any moral standing, but because I had not found a man worthy to give myself to.

After a night of club hopping, I would return to my dorm room feeling sad that I didn't have a boy to call the next day. On the nights when a boy would call me the next day, the conversation wouldn't last longer than five minutes because we had nothing of substance to talk about. One particular night, I recall coming back to my dorm room alone *again*. I felt defeated because I drank way too much, I was scantily clad in an outfit that I wouldn't want my parents to see me in, and I found myself profusely apologizing to God as I read through the Psalms. Even though my intention was to have fun, I just didn't feel comfortable with the way I was putting myself out there, dancing in a crowded bar filled with smoke and overly crude music. I felt confused because I attended a Campus for Christ ministry on Tuesday, went to Club McCoy's on Thursday, and then attended church on Sunday, confessing to God my indiscretions for that week.

I was struggling with my 'good girl' image—living a double life in a way. I was exploring my relationship with God, while trying to find love, while dancing on tables at clubs. Deep down, I knew I wasn't going to find what I was looking for at a nightclub. I knew I didn't want a one night stand or a summer fling, I wanted to be in a real relationship with just one guy for a lifetime. I just didn't know how to go about finding him.

The summer of 2002 was an end and a beginning all at the same time. It was the end of the old me and the beginning of a new one. I had been raised in church since I was a little girl, and the tenants of Christianity had always played a distant role in my life, but on my priority list, God was probably number 2,367. I felt like I was a good, moral person, but I didn't want to be associated with those crazy Bible thumping believers that accosted you as soon as you stepped out the front door. I was a "safe" Christian who believed in Jesus, but always assumed my personal life was separate from my church life. I didn't know until later that God was interested in guiding me through every area of my life.

The tugging of my heart began on a hot summer day riding in the car with my parents. My father asked me, "Have you ever publicly given your life to Jesus?"

In my head I was thinking, *why in the world is my dad asking me this question?* Of course, I believe in Jesus. I had said the prayer after all. I knew that He died on the cross for my sins, and I identified myself as a Christian. So, I didn't really see the need to make a big show of it. I was good. Yet, my dad said something that really caught my attention.

He said, "Jesus called His disciples out in a very public manner. He even said, *'but whoever denies me before men, I also will deny before my Father who is in heaven'" (Matthew 10:33, ESV).*

I stopped. I had no idea until then that it was important

to be public about my faith. Yet, as I thought about it more, I realized, if it was something I believed in, why would I be ashamed to declare it publicly? I certainly didn't want to deny Jesus. So, in part to clear my conscience and in part to please my parents, I decided that the next time we went to church, I would step out.

That day came sooner than I expected. On a clear Sunday morning, I distinctly remember Pastor James Martin of Mt. Olivet Baptist Church in Portland, Oregon saying something like, "If there is anyone who wants to give their life to Christ, come to the altar, God is waiting for you." I paused. Inside I was shaking in my boots and a million thoughts were racing through my mind. *Should I get up now? No, I can't do this. Oh gosh, I'm scared. What are they going to do to me? What does this mean? Why am I so nervous?* I sat frozen in my chair. The music played on and nobody moved. A few more seconds passed that seemed like an eternity until I heard Pastor Martin's voice again.

This time I couldn't resist the invitation. I felt myself stand up and slowly make my way to the center aisle and down the steps as I heard a thunderous applause from the congregation. All the doubts and fears I had a few seconds ago disappeared. I felt like I was finally coming home. From the moment I stood up, I knew my life was about to change forever. I had a vision of Jesus Himself sitting on His throne waiting for me at the altar and rising to meet me as a host of angels surrounded Him, cheering me on. I could almost hear Him saying, *"You have risen for Me today, now I will rise for you for the rest of your life."* I was embarking on a brand new journey, and my faith in Jesus would give me the power to do what I couldn't do before.

That summer I really did fall in love, but the person I fell in love with looked nothing like the boys I read about in romance novels. I dove deep into the Bible and its pages started to come alive in my heart. The verse from 1 John 4:19 (KJV) says, *"We love him, because he first loved us,"* rang true in my life. I discovered a relationship with the Holy Spirit as our Helper and Intercessor. I learned through my mom how to pray and talk to the Holy Spirit like I was talking to a friend. I found Him to be not just a friend that sticks closer than a brother, but a true gentleman in every sense of the word. He was patient, loving, and kind. I learned how to pray and watched in amazement as He answered those prayers.

My new relationship with God changed me

from the inside out. I felt alive, full of hope, and I developed a deep sense of purpose. I learned how real the Bible verse, *"Therefore if any man be in Christ, he is a new creature: old things are passed away; behold, all things are become new,"* (2 Corinthians 5:17, KJV) truly was. I felt like a brand new person. The seed that was planted from listening to Charles Stanley on TV two years back started to come to life. God helped me to see through His eyes that I was beautiful, special, and most of all, loved. That summer I fell in love with the one who created me, the Prince of Peace—Jesus.

Chapter 3
A Promise Made

"By night on my bed I sought him whom my soul loveth:
I sought him, but I found him not."
~Song of Solomon 3:1

After my summer of transformation, I still had the desire to be in a committed relationship with a guy, but my desire for the type of man I wanted shifted. He still needed to be cute, but he also had to love Jesus. I started to spend less time obsessing over boy bands and more time meditating on the things of God and discovering who I was in Christ. Prior to then, I had been looking for a prince to sweep me off my feet, when the whole time, the love that I was desperately searching for was right in front of me.

In this period, I learned how to recognize the voice of my Father in Heaven. I discovered that God responds in ways you will know it is Him, and no one else. Spending time in prayer, singing worship songs, and meditating on Scriptures from the Bible became my everything. It was such an incredibly freeing, transforming, and life-altering experience. I was shocked it took me so long to discover it. I found Him to be such a gentleman. He was patient, loving, affirming, and so *present*.

Even though I had so many questions, fears, and uncertainties, God held my hand each step of the way. I would ask Him questions like, *'What should I study in school LORD?'* And He would guide me. *'How do I pay my school fees LORD?'* And He would provide. *'I could use a good friend right now LORD, please help'*—and He would put amazing girlfriends in my path. I began to fall in love with who God was and everything He represented. My desire to discover what love was, from a Christ-centered perspective, far outweighed my need to find love the conventional way.

I started to think, if I was going to trust God with my life, I might as well trust Him with my love life because my way of finding love wasn't exactly working out. If I was going to look for guidance from anyone, I figured it best I entrust the Creator of the Universe. For me, that meant going back to the basics of sex education; it meant going back to the Bible. I was first introduced to the concept of sex at a young age, and although I had not personally participated in it, I was sold on the idea that sex was solely for recreation and pleasure. It didn't dawn on me that God designed sex to be expressed in the sanctity of marriage and not just for self-gratification.

As a young girl, I assumed that when you became a mature adult, or when two people were 'in love,' sex could be brought into the equation. I assumed my first time would be by candlelight, soft music and roses just like the movies. The emotional, physical, and spiritual consequences of having sex didn't really cross my mind until I made the decision to invite Christ into the equation. The more time I spent at church being taught and discipled, the more I learned that love was not just about passion and affection, it was about commitment and sacrifice. Hebrews 13:4 (KJV) says,

"Marriage is honorable in all, and the bed undefiled."

Marriage was a holy covenant. I learned from the Bible that God created marriage when He made Adam and Eve. I meditated on Scriptures like Mark 10:6-9 (KJV) that says, "But from the beginning of the creation God made them male and female. For this cause shall a man leave his father and mother, and cleave to his wife; And they two shall be one flesh: so then they are no more two, but one flesh. What therefore God hath joined together, let not man put asunder."

It dawned on me, after reading Bible verses like this, that God, not man, was doing the joining. His design was to bring two people together in holy matrimony and create one flesh. Sexual intimacy was ultimately an expression of a sacred covenant and the act of it sealed the union between husband and wife.

I even remember seeking advice from spiritual leaders on the topic and discovering God really did design sex in the context of a marriage covenant. I realized I wanted that for myself, I wanted God's best, but I wasn't sure if I could carry it out. At the time, the idea of God wanting me to save sex for marriage was completely new to me. I liked how it sounded in theory, but in reality, I wasn't fully convinced it was something I could do.

Even though I was still growing in the Christian faith, I was smart enough to know I couldn't rely on my own judgement and had to trust something or someone that was bigger than my limited worldview and experience. I also knew how fickle and boy crazy I could be. At that point, I wanted better for my life and for my future, so I made the decision to go all in. I went to my bedroom and shut the door because God and I were about to have a serious heart to heart. I said to Him, *"God, I don't fully understand this or what I am saying, but I want to approach sex Your way. I am making a promise to You to wait until marriage to give my body away because I want to please You, and I want to do this the right way. Please help me, in Jesus name, amen."*

I was a little nervous before I prayed because I wondered, *what if I don't come through, then what? What would God think of me? Wouldn't He be completely disappointed?*

I was scared that somehow I would break the promise and be riddled with guilt and regret. Right in the midst of my hesitation, I felt an amazing sense of peace that God would give me the power to wait. Every time I felt a wave of doubt, God would remind me that the reason I prayed was because of my faith and trust in

Him, and not because of my confidence in my own self. I knew that God created my body and sex was His idea, so I felt secure that He was more than able to guide me in this area.

My desire to wait on God before my first time was reaffirmed during my time in college at Concordia University, Oregon. I attended a seminar by Brad Henning about dating and relationships. During the conference, Brad said, "Love is a choice. You choose to love. Love, by definition, is choosing the highest good for the other person."

Hearing love described in that manner changed my perspective. The whole time, I was thinking about myself and how I would feel if I fell in love and how much richer my life would be. Everything was centered around my feelings and had little to do with the person I would be in a relationship with. That day, sitting in the auditorium, I learned that I could begin loving my future husband by my actions right then. I learned that what I did today, long before I even met my future spouse, would matter to him in the future. I learned it was important to guard my heart and carefully choose any relationship I might enter into, because I would be accountable for it and my behavior now could affect my relationship with my future husband. I learned that true love was choosing the highest good for your future spouse always. I read a verse in Proverbs 31:12 (KJV) that said, *"She will do him good and not evil all the days of her life."*

Knowing that inspired me to write a love letter to this future husband I hadn't even met yet. It was my way of expressing the deep desire within me to give love, and it was also a way to honor the promise I had made to God. It helped me to be accountable to my decision. That letter would be the first of many. I wrote a series of letters to my future husband dated from 2004 to 2008 and kept them tucked away safely in my room. Every time I felt discouraged about if or when I would meet the future love of my life, I would pull the letters out and pray over them. Those letters were my faith symbols, or as Hebrews 11:1 (KJV) says, *"Now faith is the substance of things hoped for, the evidence of things not seen."*

I wanted to give them to my future husband one day and tell him that I had been thinking of him long before I even met him—that I had been practicing honoring him with my heart and body before we met. I believe fidelity and loyalty are something you can build before you even enter into a season of marriage, and I wanted to build that. It is a deeply personal letter, but one I believe is important to share because it played such a pivotal role in my story:

March 25th, 2004
Dear Future Love of My Life,

So, I am writing this letter to you now, not knowing who you are yet, anticipating the day when God is going to bring us together as one. Right now, I am on a journey learning how to lean on God and learning how to trust Him when it comes to my heart—and trusting Him to write our love story. I don't know who you are, but the amazing thing is, God is building a deep love in my heart for you, I can barely contain it. I can't wait to meet you and tell you just how much you mean to me. I hope to give this letter to you on our honeymoon night, because the greatest gift I could ever hope to give you is my heart. I want to thank our LORD and Savior for granting me the grace and strength to wait for you. I thank Him for showing me that my love and faithfulness to you is a lifetime commitment that begins long before I even know who you are. Proverbs 31:12 (KJV) says, "She will do him good and not evil all the days of her life." A book I am reading now called "When God Writes Your Love Story" by Eric and Leslie Ludy, gave me an awesome revelation of what this verse means. It told me that I must seek your highest good all the days of my life, starting right now. You mean so much to me that to even think of giving my heart to another makes me sick. I want to demonstrate my love for you by guarding my heart, my soul, my body until the day when God brings us together as one. I am so grateful even now to know I will meet you someday. I am so proud to be called your wife, and so flattered that God would choose me to fulfil that position. I hope and pray that I can be the wife you have hoped and prayed for. I pray that I will love you in every way you need to be loved. I pray I can stand by your side and support you and encourage you, laugh with you, cry with you, dance with you, pray with you, support you all the days of my life.

I want you to know that when I said, "I Do" I meant it with all my heart and meant it for forever. I don't know what our future holds, but I know God holds our future. I know that I trust Him with all my heart and He is ever so faithful to His children, so He will see us through anything and everything as we keep our eyes on Him. This is the beginning of the next chapter of my life, only now it is no longer just my story, but our story. I hope that, through it all, for as many years as God blesses us to be together on this earth (and I am praying it will be a long looong time :) and as many children as we have (we'll discuss that one with God later), I hope we never lose sight of the gem we see in each other, that we never forget our calling to serve and glorify God as individuals and as man and wife.

Always and faithfully, your wife,
Mrs. Simisola _____
(I get to fill this one later- I can't wait!)

Chapter 4
The Pain of the Wait

*"I charge you, O daughters of Jerusalem, that ye stir not
up, nor awake my love, until he please."*
~Song of Solomon 8:4

I wish I could say I waited ever so patiently for a godly mate and trusted completely in God's timing. There were certainly days when I was full of faith and hope that love would find me, but most times I was anxious, doubtful, and impatient. I wanted to take my love life into my own hands.

Initially, I thought finding a godly mate would happen easily. In my mind I thought, *now that I have a relationship with God, all I have to do is pray and in no time God will answer. Out of the miracle box would pop my husband complete with a bow and confetti.* It didn't quite happen that way. The days of waiting turned into weeks, the weeks turned into months, the months turned into years with no love in sight.

I would watch my close friends get into relationships, then get out of relationships only to get into a brand new relationship the very next month. I would shake my head in disbelief. All I wanted was to be in one relationship. *How is it that Suzy Q is falling in love for the tenth time? Why is it so hard for me to find just one guy, Jesus?* At times, I thought it was all a cruel joke. I remember on many occasions complaining to my parents, asking them why I had to 'suffer' for being single. Why was it that I was doing the right thing by not giving my body away and guarding my heart, and I had absolutely nothing to show for it?

Many nights I would literally cry myself to sleep because I felt so alone and so unloved. Deep down, I knew that wasn't true. God loved me; His Word promised never to leave me or forsake me. My faith knew that, but my flesh reacted otherwise. I was alone on another Friday night. Again.

There were also times when I looked to other Jesus loving Christian singles, hoping they would somehow motivate me to stay the path and wait on God for my perfect mate. The examples were few and far between. Some of my friends who had expressed to me their intention to wait until marriage quickly changed their minds as soon as they entered a serious relationship. I even started to look to famous Christian celebrities who were single, in hopes they could be my shining example of what it meant to wait patiently on God. I would have a twinge of hope as I listened to them make public declarations of their intention to save sex for marriage, only to watch them being photographed half-dressed leaving a hotel room with their significant other, their purity ring nowhere in sight. I was discouraged. I would think to myself, *God, I made a promise to you to remain a virgin until marriage. Lord, I am struggling right now. I see all these people around me giving in and having so much fun with their sexual freedom. What makes me think I can hang on? In fact, why am I even hanging on? What is the point?*

My dad would encourage me in those times,

telling me not to worry and to continue to be patient because in God's economy, the last shall be first. My dad, in his fatherly wisdom, would say, "Don't worry about dating so many people, after all, you only want to marry one person, not 300."

My dad was right. I knew if I wanted to be with *any* guy I could. I could easily just walk into a bar and respond to the first guy who showed interest in me. The truth was, I didn't want to pick just anybody off the shelf. I wanted something deeper. In all the times when I felt hopeless, God would always send someone to remind me that I didn't want to be with just any guy; I wanted to be with the right one.

Overall, waiting on Mr. Wonderful was taking a little longer than I thought. Every year on January 1st, I would think, *this will be the year love finds me.* It was my secret New Year's resolution. By mid-June, I was still holding on to the hope of a summer romance. By September, I would convince myself that love was just around the corner. When December rolled around, I would slip into a slight depressive funk over the fact that I was still single.

I graduated with an undergraduate degree in college with no boyfriend. Then, I started working full-time—still no boyfriend. At this point, I started to believe something was seriously wrong with me. I was convinced I was abnormal, an anomaly of some sort. I went back to school to get my master's degree and thought surely love would find me. I was wrong. I watched my friends transition from serious relationships to engagements, to marriage. I felt so left out. Even though I had a master's degree, I felt like a kindergartner in the area of love. Everybody and their grandmother was in a relationship, and I was convinced I was subject to become a spinster for life.

My impatience rose to such a level that I actually considered becoming a nun. For a whole afternoon, I researched the possibility of joining a nunnery. Mother Theresa was a nun, so why not me? Being married to Jesus couldn't be so bad, could it? Yet the more I researched, the more I realized I couldn't picture a life without my husband by my side, without children to call my own. Something in my gut told me I was called into marriage and motherhood. I knew there was nothing wrong with being single, if that was what I was graced to do. Unfortunately, I didn't have the gift of singleness like Paul of Tarsus, so becoming a nun for me was out of the question. As much as I adored Jesus, I couldn't deny I wanted to feel a human touch: and I for one, most certainly did not want to die a virgin.

By the end of that afternoon, I concluded I would just have to keep waiting, so help me God.

Chapter 5
A Fleece Laid

"I am the rose of Sharon, and the lily of the valleys."
~Song of Solomon 2:1

"God did you notice how cute that guy was? And oh, how he lifted his hands to worship You in church? He must be 'the one.' I am certain of it. In fact, God I believe I heard your voice speaking." Of course, the voice I was hearing was not God's voice, but wishful thinking from my own heart. There were so many guys I had a crush on, and unfortunately, I quickly misinterpreted a crush to mean, "match made in heaven." I quickly discovered crushes were designed to do exactly what the word stated, crush you.

During my single days, I spent a lot of time thinking about how I could go about selecting my future spouse. I had been wrong so many times about guys I liked who I thought could be "the one" and wondered, how was I going to know when I actually met the one? Was it supposed to be trial and error? A guessing game? Was I supposed to wait for one guy to break my heart before I proceeded to the next? I didn't want to have to kiss fifty frogs to find my prince. I knew the only person who could help me was God.

Around 2006, a friend told me a story about how God was very specific in answering prayers, even down to the color and number of flowers. A girl had been praying for guidance for a future spouse, and in order to spare confusion, she prayed that God would show her if the person she was dating was the one by having him bring a single white rose to her door when they went on a date. She dated a few people and one guy even brought a dozen red roses to her door. The relationship didn't work out for various reasons. One day, a different guy she was talking to brought a single white rose to her door and her heart leaped. God had heard! They ended up getting married and starting a beautiful life together. That story sparked something in me. I wondered, does God care about the details of our lives? Does He really delight in answering our prayers, even down to the last minutia?

I wanted to have crazy faith like that girl. I began to think, what would it look like if I really trusted God to pick the man for me? How could I pray? I was inspired by the story of Gideon in Judges 6. God sent an angel to Gideon and told him that he was chosen to rescue his people, the Israelites, from the oppressive hand of the Midianites, who were basically starving them to death. At the point when the angel came, Gideon felt abandoned by God. He also felt weak and inadequate. He said to the angel, "How can I rescue Israel? My clan is the weakest in the whole tribe of Manasseh, and I am the least in my entire family!" God reassured Gideon not to worry, but to trust that He would be with him. So, Gideon asked God for a sign saying, "If you are truly going to use me to rescue Israel, as you promised, prove it to me in this way. I will put a wool fleece on the threshing floor tonight. If the fleece is wet with dew in the morning, but the ground is dry, then I will know that you are going to help me rescue Israel as you promised."

The next morning, Gideon woke up and found the fleece sopping wet and the ground completely dry, just as he had asked. God had given Gideon a sign to reassure him that he was moving in the right direction. In the same way, I felt inspired to lay out my own fleece before God. I wanted God to guide me in the area of marriage by asking Him to show me, and to confirm it with a sign like He did for Gideon.

I began to imagine what my ideal date would look like. What would I want to do with the man I would marry on our very first date? For me, my sign was simple and sweet: ice cream. For our first date, I didn't want to go to a movie, or to a fancy restaurant or even a coffee shop. When I pictured my first date, I saw myself sitting down with a yummy bowl of ice-cream and enjoying great conversation. I shared my heart with my heavenly Father and told Him I wanted my first date with my future husband to be over a bowl of ice-cream. I prayed a dangerous prayer filled with hope and expectation. I said, "God, would you confirm who the one for me is by having him take me out for ice cream on our first date?"

I knew in my heart it was a radical prayer, but I also had a deep trust that God hears when we come to Him in faith. The Bible says, *"But without faith it is impossible to please him: for he that cometh to God must believe that he is, and that he is a rewarder of them that diligently seek him" (Hebrews 11:6, KJV).* I felt so much peace in laying out my fleece like Gideon and relying on the God of the universe to guide me.

Chapter 6
I Had A Dream

"I sleep, but my heart waketh: it is the voice of my beloved that knocketh, saying, Open to me, my sister, my love." ~Song of Solomon 5:2

Years went by and nothing happened. I started to wonder if my prayer would ever be answered. Yet every time I felt low, something would happen to encourage my faith to keep believing, keep trusting in God's timing, and keep waiting.

One night, I had a dream I will never forget. It was as though God was sending me a dream ahead of time to prepare my heart for what was about to take place. I recorded it in my journal on January 17th, 2010:

It was nighttime in a theatre venue, I was about to be introduced to a lot of potential suitors and was supposed to pick the one I was interested in. At first, I didn't want to because I had seen the guys from a distance and none of them caught my attention. Also, I was a little embarrassed because my colleagues, Holly and Erica, and others were watching. The director of CBN International was also at the entrance of the door, and I asked him for his advice. He said to me, "Lay out your fleece like Gideon." I was puzzled at first, but then I realized he was telling me to give it a chance and ask God to direct me to the right one. I came closer to the guys who were on stage and my eyes zoned in on one of the guys standing there. Somehow, in my heart, I knew there was something there. I felt as though God wanted me to test His word, to know for sure this was the right guy for me. I was to ask the question that only God would know the answer to and reveal the one that was for me. I took a nervous breath and posed this question to all the guys:

"If you were to take me out on a date for the first time, where would you take me?"

The guy with dark brown hair answered, "I would take you out for ice cream."

My heart soared, and I remember feeling like I wanted to drop to the ground in amazement at God's preciseness and relief that He had remembered my fleece. God was guiding me to the one and giving me the desire of my heart. I may have actually dropped to the ground.

In the dream, he was even more attractive the closer I got. We hugged in complete confidence that we were made for each other.

He then gave me a beautiful ring that had many colors on it (almost like a rainbow) and put it on my hand. It wasn't an engagement ring, yet I knew he would give me one soon. The ring was bright, unique, and symbolized the uniqueness of our relationship, the hope of the future, and his love for me. Afterwards, he went backstage to help other guys move furniture without being asked. After some time, I came backstage and was wondering how a girlfriend was to behave. I didn't feel the need to call him to see where he was. I felt secure in our relationship.

Dreams have played a pivotal role in my Christian walk, and I have seen on numerous occasions how God has given me dreams to guide me, forewarn me, or give me hope of a future to come. The Bible says in Job 33:15 (KJV), *"For God speaketh once, yea twice, yet man perceiveth it not. In a dream, in a vision of the night, when deep sleep falleth upon men, in slumberings upon the bed."* Having this dream gave me a sense of reassurance that I was on the right track. I was inspired to write a poem describing the person I sensed he would be:

Waiting For the Ice Cream Man

If I were to imagine you, the best you,
Without knowing who you are
If I were to imagine you, without constrictions-
The man I would love to marry
If I were to imagine you, the best you,
Who would I see?
I would see deep into your eyes
A well of love, kindness, and strength
I would see deeply into your soul
And recognize the peace of Christ.
I would see a quiet strength—
Thoughtful yet bold.
I would see an ocean of laughter,
So much laughter, so much joy.
I would see the hottest man on earth-
A deep physical attraction whose foundation
Is secured by an even deeper soul connection.
You have a killer smile and a twinkle in your eye.
Your hands are big and warm
And fit perfectly in mine.
With you we have constant exploration
We fall in love with the Father all over again,
Again and again and again.
Why?
Because in each other we realize that He has done
Exceedingly, abundantly, above and beyond all we
Could ask, think, or imagine in our marriage.
We love you Lord!

Years later, I would look back on my dreams and visions from this time in wonder because everything unfolded just as God had showed me. I can testify that God is most certainly a fulfiller of every single one of His promises.

Chapter 7
Almost Doesn't Count

"I will rise now, and go about the city in the streets, and in the broad ways I will seek him whom my soul loveth: I sought him, but I found him not."
~Song of Solomon 3:2

There was a saying I was all too familiar with: almost doesn't count. In the season right before I met my husband, I met a lot of *'almosts.'* There were times I would be introduced to a seemingly nice guy who had most of the qualities I liked, but something would always be off. Well-meaning family members and friends would attempt to set me up with a guy they thought was perfect for me, and I would have phone conversations with them, but it never went further than that. I would enjoy our initial conversation, and hope something more would develop, but something would inevitably come up that made me feel as though, if I continued any further, I would be settling. In those times, the wise words of my uncle would spring into my heart, "*Wait, don't settle.*"

Trust me when I say, on many occasions, I was tempted to settle. I wanted to ignore the red flag of the guy I noticed who enjoyed partying a little too much. I was also tempted to settle for a guy who didn't think going to church every Sunday was important. I was tempted to settle for mediocre even though something in my spirit knew God had something great.

I remember a particular guy, who I'd talked to a few times over the phone, that I really seemed to vibe with. A good friend of mine connected us via Facebook, and I found him to be funny, warm, and I was drawn to the fact that he enjoyed working with children. I had not met him in person, but from his pictures, I could tell he was tall and handsome. I discovered that he liked different cultures and seemed to be really interested in getting to know me. He would text me things like, "Good morning beautiful," and "How was your day gorgeous?" I thought to myself, maybe this could turn into something meaningful.

Initially, it seemed as though I had green lights in every area, and I started to get excited. I was hopeful, but still very guarded. So, I prayed, sincerely asking God to show me this guy's heart. Boy did God answer that prayer. Everything lined up perfectly *except* our views on faith. Even then, I kept talking to him, hoping in the few weeks that we were talking, he would have a spiritual epiphany and declare his undying passion and commitment to Jesus so we could proceed to planning our wedding.

The exact opposite happened. In fact, God made things so clear to me during one of our conversations; he decided we should play the 10-Question game. I remembered the dream God had given me concerning my ice cream fleece and thought this was a perfect opportunity to test him to see what his answer would be. For my first question I asked, "If you could take me out on our first date where would you take me?" His answer caught me completely off guard.

"McDonald's. I would take you to McDonald's." The conversation should have ended after that response, but I was still holding out hope and thought to myself, *they sell ice cream at McDonald's. Maybe he will buy me ice cream there.* I hadn't even finished the thought when he said, "I hate ice cream. I can't stand it."

I chuckled internally thinking what a great sense of humor God has. It was abundantly clear this guy was never taking me out for ice cream. I knew, without a shadow of a doubt, that I could not settle for this guy. Yet, even as I battled with a final decision on whether to continue talking to him, he asked me his tenth and final question. I believe this was God's way of making it abundantly clear this was not the man for me.

He said, "Do you believe in sex after marriage or before?" *What kind of question is that dude?* I thought to myself. *The fact that you are even asking me this question tells me everything I need to know.* I told him flatly, "After marriage."

He then proceeded to dissertate on the benefits of sex before marriage saying things like, "How else will you know if the sex is good, if you don't give it a test run?"

I told him emphatically, "If the person is your first sexual encounter, you have no one else to compare them to. Besides, once you are married, you have your whole lifetime to practice and get it right."

After that conversation, he could tell I had closed off completely. I respectfully told him I wasn't interested in continuing the conversation. He seemed a little confused, but I knew I could never explain it to him in a way that he could fully understand. How could I tell him that he had failed the Ice Cream Test?

A part of me was sad that I was so adamant on sticking to my values and refusing to compromise. I was genuinely disappointed that things didn't work out between us. I was a virgin not because I didn't have emotions or desires to be with a man. I was a virgin because I didn't want to give my heart or body away to someone I wasn't in a marital covenant with.

Truth be told, even though I was a virgin in body, I still struggled with thoughts and fantasies. I had to learn how to be honest and open with God about those thoughts and allow Him to guide me away from them so that I wasn't tempted to act on them.

The Bible verse from 1 Corinthians 10:13 became my lifeline on many occasions. It says, "*There hath no temptation taken you but such as is common to man: but God is faithful, who will not suffer you to be tempted above that ye are able; but will with the temptation also make a way to escape, that ye may be able to bear it*" (*1 Corinthians 10:13, KJV*).

There was one occasion during my third year of college where the verses of that Scripture came to life. I went to a campus basketball game with a guy that I met in class, and he offered to walk me back to my dorm. Something in my gut told me this was not a good idea, but I ignored it. Before we made it to my building, he told me he needed to grab something from his dorm room first and invited me inside. Another alarm bell went off inside my head, but I pushed it aside again.

We stepped inside his room and he shut the door. *This is a really bad idea,* I thought. He sat on his bed and invited me to sit down next to him. I immediately got a sinking feeling in my heart, not because I was afraid of him, but because I was afraid of what might happen next. The Bible verse from Corinthians popped into my mind. *God always provides a way of escape.* I silently prayed, *"Oh Lord please help me out of this one!"* As soon as the words left my lips, his phone rang. Thank you, Jesus! I thought.

It was one of his friends who needed his attention urgently. He told me to wait in his room, and he would be right back. The minute he left, I had enough sense to know this was my way out. I took advantage of the window of time I was given and bolted out of his room as fast as I could. He didn't hear from me again after that night.

Following that incident, I made a conscious effort to identify the triggers that would lead me to daydream about getting romantic with a guy and make a sincere effort to avoid them.

One of my triggers, for example, was watching love scenes that featured an actor I thought was really cute. When the kissing scene would begin, I would close my eyes and turn my head, or press fast-forward, or sometimes even leave the room. This was my way of being radical about guarding not only my body but my heart. I knew it was only by the grace of God that I had remained a virgin for this long, and I took the advice from Jesus when he said in Matthew 18:9 (KJV), *"And if thine eye offend thee, pluck it out, and cast it from thee: it is better for thee to enter into life with one eye, rather than having two eyes to be cast into hell fire."*

Thankfully, in my moments of weakness, I didn't allow myself to get stuck in a room with a really cute guy because who knows what could have happened. During all the times I was tempted to settle, something in my spirit reminded me that God had so much in store for me if I could just hold on and trust Him.

Chapter 8
A Taste For Vanilla

"How beautiful you are, my darling! Oh, how beautiful!"

Song of Solomon 1:15

Tuesday August 23rd, 2011 is a day I will never forget. It is the reason I am writing this book. It is a testimony to the fact that God does care about our deepest prayers, and He is in the business of answering them. The morning of August 23rd, 2011 started out like any other day, yet by the end of the day, I could hardly pick my jaw up off the ground because of what God had done.

Before I get to the events of that day, I must begin with the year prior when I met a guy named Samuel at Realm of Glory Church, Abuja. He was the Music Director at the time, and I remember really enjoying the worship and chatting briefly with him afterwards. A few days later, he called me and told me he got my number from my cousin Seun. During our conversation, Samuel talked about his passion for music, and I talked to him about my work as a TV Producer with *Turning Point International*. The conversation was extremely neutral, and I genuinely thought he was calling to connect with me for networking purposes. I was happy to do so, and we exchanged Facebook info. He seemed like a nice guy, and I wished him all the best. Developing a romantic relationship with him was the furthest thing from my mind because I had no interest in living in Nigeria and didn't even entertain the possibility of taking the conversation further. Looking back on that time, I am so glad God didn't give me a clue about what would take place the following year.

A year passed and I went on a work trip to

Ghana to produce some stories for *Turning Point International.* My parents suggested I come to Nigeria after I was done with work since it would just be a quick flight from Accra to Abuja. I was happy to do so because I loved any opportunity I had to spend time with my parents. It's funny to think back on my time in Ghana because I remember my friend and fellow producer, Erica, jokingly saying, "What if you meet your husband there?" I laughed and told her, "No way! I refuse to marry a Nigerian."

Boy was I wrong.

On August 23rd, 2011, I had planned to spend the day with my parents to gather documents needed for my Nigerian passport. The process was expected to take the whole day, so I was bracing myself for the inevitable hours I would spend waiting in line. That morning Samuel, the same guy I talked to a year prior, called asking me whether I had plans that day because he wanted to show me around Abuja. I genuinely felt like he was being hospitable because I was new to the area, and he just wanted to help me feel more at home. Just a few days before, Sam came to me after church and told me that he had asked my father if he could show me around town when he learned I would be coming to visit.

When I relayed the conversation to my dad, he told me he had forgotten to mention it to me. Truth be told, my mind was focused on another guy. I was genuinely waiting for the other guy to officially ask me out, but that hadn't happened yet, and I was really frustrated about it. The morning of August 23rd, after Sam asked me what my plans were, my initial reaction was to brush him off. But for some reason, my theatre dream came to mind and I sensed the Holy Spirit telling me to be open to the possibility of developing a friendship with Sam. So instead of brushing him off, I told him that day was going to be extremely busy for me, and I wasn't sure if I would have time to hang out with him, but I would be in touch and let him know.

On that Tuesday, we went to the passport office and were sent on a wild goose chase to so many locations I lost count. Anyone who knows Nigeria, knows how difficult it can be to obtain the necessary paperwork for a passport. I lost hope that we would be done that day, so I called Sam and apologetically told him I most likely would have to cancel. The gracious way he answered when I told him I was changing plans really caught my attention. He was easy-going, patient, and kind. I appreciated how understanding he was, and I felt a small part of my heart start to open up.

Angels must have been working on our behalf that day because we completed the passport paperwork a lot earlier than I originally thought. I decided to call Sam back to let him know that my schedule had opened up. Again, he was gracious, warm, and kind. He told me he would come pick me up at my parents' house. I knew from our earlier conversation that he also had a busy day, yet he made a point to set our meeting as a priority. That was endearing to me.

As I began to get ready in the bathroom, I couldn't shake the feeling that there was something special about this day and something really special about Sam. I wanted to ignore the feeling because I had made up my mind I was not going to date anybody in Nigeria, yet despite my internal protests, I had a strong witness in my spirit that God was about to move. Today was the day.

I remember kneeling down on the bathroom floor and praying, *"God I don't know why I am having this strong feeling about Samuel like You are about to do something. Whatever it is, not my will but Your will be done."*

Sam walked into my parents' house moments later wearing a dark green native African Kaftan.

I looked down at my dark green print dress and immediately noticed we were matching. This was going to be quite the night, I could already tell.

At the point when we left my parent's house, I still had no idea where he was taking me. During our earlier conversation, he had mentioned going to the shopping mall or for a movie, but since it was later in the day, I wondered if his plans had changed. We pulled up to the parking lot of what I would later learn was Ceddi Plaza mall. As we walked up the escalator of the mall, I asked Sam, "What do you like to do when you come here?" He listed a bunch of activities, and honestly, I don't remember all of them because everything became a blur as soon as he mentioned ice cream.

Oh my goodness, he likes ice cream? I thought. My heart was beating fast, but then it slowed down when I thought, *just because he mentioned ice cream does not mean he is about to buy it.* I was determined not to read into anything.

Sam guided me to one of the floors in the mall, and as we were walking, I noticed a food store with an ice cream kiosk in front of us. My heart skipped a beat, and I thought, *is this really happening?* Sam led me right past the ice cream shop, and we walked a distance until we reached some tables and chairs. He pulled out a chair for me to sit down on. I breathed a sigh of relief. *Okay, we are not having ice cream, this is good. I can relax now.*

Sam proceeded to tell me how much he enjoyed getting to know my father and how much my dad had encouraged him in his music ministry. We talked about our goals and dreams. He shared his heart for music and missions, and living a life that gave glory to God. I shared with him about my desire to minister to people through media and writing. I felt immediately at ease as we talked. It was almost as though we had known each other all our lives; the conversation flowed so easily. I almost forgot where we were until Sam jumped up and told me he wanted to get me something to eat from the food store—*that also happened to sell ice cream.*

As we walked over to the shop, he looked at me and said, "Tell me, what would you like to eat?"

I stood frozen. I was at a loss of what to say, and I couldn't get over the fact that we were actually standing in a snack store that sold ice cream.

"What would you like to eat?" Sam's deep voice interrupted my thoughts.

"Uh, I don't know, you tell me."

"No, really get whatever you want," Sam said.

"Um, I don't know," I said. "How about you pick?" I knew my behavior wasn't making any sense, but I couldn't very well tell him the reason for my hesitation. In my mind, I was thinking, *I can't pick because I need to know if you will pass my fleece test. This date and our future is entirely contingent upon what you buy me.*

At that point, Sam looked slightly puzzled as to why I couldn't seem to make up my mind, but he was gracious as usual. He proceeded towards one of the servers to look at the menu, then he asked for some meat pies and cookies. I stood behind him as he made the order, again feeling relief that he wasn't buying ice cream. His voice interrupted my thoughts when I heard him, clear as day, say, "Ice cream."

He looked towards the left where the ice cream was sitting behind the glass. My eyes bulged. I was standing behind him and thankful he couldn't see the look on my face. *This is the second time he has mentioned ice cream today. Why does he keep saying ice cream, LORD? Please make this abundantly clear Jesus!* I was profusely praying under my breath. At that point, Sam turned around and walked to my right where there was a fridge full of drinks. He grabbed a drink, then closed the fridge door. Holding the drink, meat pies, and cookies, he led me towards the counter where he pulled out his wallet to pay for the items.

I'm in the clear now, I thought. *It was just a coincidence that he had mentioned ice cream before, he's not actually going to buy me ice cream.*

I hadn't even finished processing my thoughts when he looked at me and said, "Don't you want ice cream?"

I was shocked. He didn't even wait for my answer before he turned back to the ice cream section and said, "I am getting you ice cream." Sam ordered two cups of vanilla (which happened to be my favorite flavor), and then returned to the checkout counter to pay for everything. I was in complete awe and disbelief that God indeed had heard. He had answered my prayer. My ice cream fleece had been fulfilled right before my eyes.

By the end of our date, Sam pulled out a camera and asked someone to take a picture of us sitting in the middle of Ceddi Plaza, with our cups of ice cream resting on the table. It was almost as if God was behind the scenes orchestrating it all, knowing that one day I would have a tangible picture to remember one of the most special days of my life—my very first date with my ice cream man.

That evening, I was scheduled to speak to the youth at Sam's church and my message was "Get Out of The Boat." I talked about stepping out in faith like Peter and watching God do the impossible in your life. In my mind, I couldn't help but make a comparison to my own situation. From the way things were going with Sam, God was leading me to get out of the boat and trust Him in this relationship. That evening, Sam was also there supporting me and being such a gracious gentleman. I remember watching him, and I noticed the servant he was to everyone around him. My heart started to open up even more.

At the time, Sam had no clue about my ice cream fleece. I prayed and said to God, "If this is really You, then I know you will confirm it through Samuel. I am not going to be the one pursuing him."

Over the next few days Sam and I chatted on the phone, texting encouraging Scriptures back and forth to each other. The more we communicated, the more he was growing on me. I just felt so comfortable with him and had such a peace that God would speak through Sam if he truly was the man for me.

The confirmation came sooner than I expected. I returned to Ghana to catch my scheduled flight back to

Virginia. At that point, Sam hadn't made his intentions known or expressed specific interest in me, but we were still communicating via text message. In my heart, I wondered, *if he really is my ice cream man, how will You bring us together God?* In my own reasoning, it seemed impossible because we lived in two different continents. I had just finished telling my colleagues that I would not consider dating someone who lived in Nigeria only two weeks prior, and here I was thinking about building a future with Sam. I continued to pray and decided that I was going to trust in the LORD and not lean on my own understanding.

When I arrived at the airport, I discovered my American return flight had been cancelled due to a tropical storm in the US. Things were backed up so badly, it would be almost a week before the next flight was available back to Virginia. I had a dilemma. *Do I stay in Ghana, or get another plane ticket and return to Nigeria to spend my 27th birthday with family and possibly see where things go with Sam?* My dad was gracious enough to stay up all night looking for a last-minute ticket for me. Most flights had been delayed or cancelled due to the tropical storm, but miraculously, he found a ticket for me, so I hopped on a plane and returned to Nigeria.

The very next day, Sam called me and took me on a walk I will never forget. We circled a neighborhood around my parents' home in Asokoro and Sam opened up to me about his feelings for me. He told me that the first time he saw me in 2010, he was drawn to me. He said he prayed asking God to bring me back to Nigeria if I was indeed the woman for him. In that moment, Sam took my hand and said, "If God would permit, I would like to spend the rest of my life with you." His words took my breath away because right before he spoke, I heard an impression in my heart from the Holy Spirit telling me to say yes to Sam's proposal. It had only been 1 week from our first date, but hearing Sam share his heart with me was all the confirmation I needed.

I journaled about my feelings a few days before my 27th birthday.

August 27th, 2011
Samuel called me in Ghana :) He is so sweet, so thoughtful, I am growing more fond of him by the day. I still have my guard up because I want to walk in Your perfect will Abba. Samuel is proving himself to be an amazing man. He is warm, funny, and he has a beautiful spirit about him. What I like most about him is his heart for You. The love he has for You is pure, genuine, and it's contagious. I am most drawn to him when he is worshipping You. I think what truly captured my heart is when he began to sing "Holy." Your glory was so heavy in the atmosphere, I wanted to drop down on

my knees and begin to worship. Daddy, I am in awe of the ways Sam is passing every test and doing everything I have longed and desired for.

1) He asked my father for permission to take me out.
2) He took me out for ice cream on our first date.
3)He is a man after Your own heart- a worshipper in spirit and in truth.
4) He has a giving heart and a heart for the poor.
5) He loves to dance :)
6) He is fun loving and free-spirited.
7) He is a man of his word. Every time he tells me he is going to do something, he does it.
8) He places God above all and encourages me to draw closer to You Abba (a million brownie points).
9) My parents love him.
10) He treats me like a princess and spoils me rotten with beautiful words of encouragement, showers me with gifts, affection, and his time.
11) He remembers everything I say—even things I've forgotten I said—and goes above and beyond the call of duty to help and support me. For example, I asked for (actually I told him I liked certain praise songs, and he bought me 18 CDs and 2 books for my b-day).
12) He is a psalmist like David.
13) Did I mention he is tall, dark, and handsome and has an anointed voice?
14) Today, he told me he wrote me a song.

Conclusion: I can trust Samuel Okai with my heart <3

I later discovered Samuel means, "God has heard," and was even more encouraged to know that, through my journey of singleness and praying and waiting, God had heard and given me my Samuel.

A few days after we were officially courting, he asked me, "Are you sure you want to be with a poor church boy like me?" Sam felt like he had nothing to offer me besides his love and commitment to the things of God.

"I am sure," I said.

For me, Sam's love for Jesus was everything. I had always prayed to be with a man who had a heart after God's heart, and Sam was that man. I knew that I could trust him with my heart.

Chapter 9
Long Distance Love

"Where has your beloved gone, most beautiful of
women? Which way did your beloved turn, that
we may look for him with you?"
~ Song of Solomon 6:1

S am and I courted long distance, and he officially proposed to me on May 23rd, 2012 in the same church building where we first met - Realm of Glory Church in Abuja Nigeria. Dating long distance was hard, but it also helped us to truly get to know each other and develop a foundation of communication and trust.

Every Wednesday, we would pray and fast together cross continentally, until I had the opportunity to travel back to Nigeria. We completed a pre-marriage counseling course at our church in Abuja. Those times were invaluable in creating a solid foundation for our relationship. During our talks over the phone, we went back and forth about whether I should relocate to Nigeria or Sam should move to the United States. After much waiting and prayer, God asked us to trust Him to make a way for Sam to move to Virginia Beach. In fact, we walked in so much faith that we solidified plans for our September 2nd wedding before even knowing whether or not Sam would get approval for a U.S. visa. The night before his visa interview, I couldn't sleep. I stayed up all night praying. At that point, our wedding venue was booked, our bridal party had purchased plane tickets, our cake was ordered, the hotel where our wedding guests would stay was reserved, and Sam's visa was not even approved yet. If Sam was denied the visa, all our plans would crumble right before our eyes. We had nothing but our faith in God to lean on.

I recorded that time in a journal entry:

It is 12:07 am Friday August 3rd, 2012, the date of Sam's interview at the U.S. embassy in Lagos, Nigeria for a K-1 Fiancé Visa. I am sitting in my prayer closet praising and thanking God for His wonders. By faith, I believe that in a few hours Samuel will call me telling me that his visa was approved, and he will be getting on Air France on August 15th to come to America and marry me. We have operated completely by faith in this entire relationship.

• *By faith, Sam proposed to me 6 days after our first date.*

• *By faith, we entered a serious and committed relationship after spending less than two weeks together in the beginning of our courtship.*

• *By faith, Sam made his intentions known to my parents and asked for my hand in marriage.*

• *By faith, I asked God to show me who my spouse would be by causing him to take me out for ice cream on our first date.*

• *Sam took me out for ice cream on our very first date, and we even took pictures that day.*

• *By faith, Sam and I chose Wednesday to fast and pray together in different time zones and continents, and I have seen You do astounding things for us and our loved ones.*

• *By faith, I wrote on a Post-it, before we saw these things come to pass, "Samuel's visa was approved, hallelujah to Jesus."*

• *Habakkuk 2 says, write down the revelation and make it plain. By faith, I booked and reserved our wedding venue at the Crystal Springs Rhododendron Gardens early in 2012 even before I had received an answer from our 1-129 Fiancé Visa.*

• *By faith, we also booked my ticket to Oregon for my wedding and Sam's return ticket from Portland to Virginia Beach.*

• *By faith, God provided a home for Sam and I beginning September 1st, 2012.*

God has already done incredible things for Sam and I by faith. He watches over His word to perform it, so I know that God has gone ahead and leveled every single mountain, cut through the bars of bronze, and the bars of iron for Sam and I. Every giant we have faced has been defeated, and every mountain we will face has already been destroyed by faith. In this visa, God will, "open doors before him so the gates will not be shut."
God has promised and He will do it. By faith, our marriage will be bound by love, faithfulness, truth, openness, intimacy of Christ, and each other. By faith, nothing will come between us and no man or woman will put asunder what God has joined together. By faith we will be bright and shining stars for God's glory.

I wrote all of these things down in my journal as a reminder of what God had already done during our courtship as I waited to hear what the verdict on Sam's visa was. I had to remind myself of God's past faithfulness and trust that He was faithful to complete the work He began in our relationship. I fell asleep with my face buried in my journal and was jolted awake by Sam's phone call from Nigeria early that morning telling me what I knew all along by faith, his visa was approved!

Chapter 10–
A New Name

"Thou hast ravished my heart, my sister, my spouse;
thou hast ravished my heart with one of thine eyes,
with one chain of thy neck."
~Song of Solomon 4:9

Samuel indeed travelled to America on August 15th, 2012 and operation name change was complete on September 2nd, 2012 when we said, "I do," and I officially became Mrs. Simisola Okai. We got married at the Crystal Springs Rhododendron

Gardens in Portland, Oregon followed by an outside reception on a glorious Sunday morning. I wanted to get married in a garden because the garden was where the first wedding took place. It was where God formed Adam and his wife Eve, the flesh of his flesh and the bone of his bones. It took a village of pastors to marry us, something my friends tease me about to this day. We felt so honored that people with spiritual authority came together from all over the world just to bless our day. God was present in every detail of the planning of my wedding, and I owe a huge debt of gratitude to my parents, my family, and my friends for their support.

Even before the wedding day, I saw God's hand of favor working everything together seamlessly, right down to how I found my Cinderella dress. Months earlier, I spent the day in New York City with my sister Teniola. The plan was to attend a church service at Hillsong, NYC, then hang around the city for a little while before going our separate ways. We both planned to spend just half a day in the city because I had a bus to catch that was returning to Virginia Beach by 3:30pm.

After an amazing church service, we decided to google Kleinfelds bridal boutique because we were curious to know where it was located. I wasn't planning on wedding dress shopping that day and just wanted to see what the outside of the store looked like. Kleinfelds was where one of my favorite shows, "Say Yes To The Dress" was filmed, and for years I had watched the show imagining what it would be like when I found "the" dress. Even before I met Sam, I had already pictured and planned what kind of dress I wanted to walk down the aisle in. I even had it down to the designer and style – a Maggie Sottero ball gown.

When my sister and I googled Kleinfeld's, we discovered it was just a few blocks away from Hillsong Church, NYC. My sister said, "Why don't we go there and see what it's like inside?"

When she said that, I looked at the time and it was 1:15 pm or so. I had to be at the bus station by 3:15pm. I wondered, *should I even risk it?*

As I stood thinking about what I should do, I looked into my sister's eyes and something leaped in my spirit. It was a *carpe diem* moment, and I knew I couldn't let this opportunity pass by. I had always wanted my sister to be there with me when I tried on wedding dresses for the first time, especially since we lived so far away from each other. I thought, *Why not? At least I will have the moment of trying on my first dress with her.*

I didn't actually plan on purchasing a dress that afternoon, but that is exactly what happened. In the blink of an eye, we located the Kleinfeld's store, and I found myself in a dressing room trying on a gorgeous silk dress that I really liked. We were having so much fun, but at that point I wasn't shopping seriously because I had convinced myself we were just playing dress up. I asked my bridal gown consultant if they had a sample Maggie Sottero dress that I could look at. I didn't think they would actually have one in my size, but when she came back and hung a gorgeous Maggie Sottero *Desdemona* dress in front of me, I had the same feeling I felt right before I went on my first date with Sam.

Uh oh.

I slipped the dress on and immediately fell in love with it. The sample size gown fit perfectly, and also happened to be on sale. I walked out of my dressing room and stepped out to a dress stand where I saw my reflection in front of a wall of mirrors.

I wanted to cry.

"This is it," I said. "I am saying yes to this dress!"

My sister loved it on me too, and I think I may have seen a tear in her eye as I walked around the room.

I couldn't believe I had found my dress in under one hour. I purchased the gown and walked out of the store, wedding dress in hand. I actually carried it on my lap during the seven-hour bus ride back to Virginia Beach. I could hardly believe my dreams were coming to life. The wait was over, and my time had come.

On that beautiful September day, the day of my wedding, I remember looking up at the stunning backdrop of trees softly swaying, and the sun beaming down on us in all its glory. It was such a moment of fulfilment to sense the presence and peace of God on my wedding day. My dad walked me down the aisle to the song, "Great is Thy Faithfulness," and placed me in the arms of Sam, who stood waiting at the altar with a huge smile on his face. That day I really did feel like Cinderella in my huge sparkly white wedding dress that fit like a glove. It was better than the story books, better than I could have ever imagined.

As someone who adores spending time with family, my heart was so full so see the people I loved gathered all around me. Our family and friends travelled from all over the U.S. and all over world—Nigeria, Australia, the United Kingdom—just to share this special day with Sam and I. During our reception,

Sam sang a beautiful song to me called "You and I." I will never forget the moment he looked deeply into my eyes and sang, "You and I will be as One. Our love will last forever. You and I, You and I. You and I will be as One."

It was quite a day—the day I had waited for all my life. There were so many funny, unplanned moments—like the fact that they initially brought us the wrong wedding cake, and then we discovered later that Sam and I were supposed to leave the wedding in a limousine that was waiting for us, but we hopped into our tiny little rental car and drove off together, completely oblivious. I suppose it was an early lesson on marriage. So many things happen that you never plan, but you learn to keep your eyes fixed on Jesus and allow Him to help you navigate the best route.

I was always taught to plan more for your marriage than you do your wedding day and found that to be so true. Although our wedding day was a glorious day, it was only a moment that marked the beginning of our lives together. We had to work out the hard stuff afterwards, like the fact that we didn't plan a honeymoon get away, and instead spent the day at the beach twenty minutes from our house. What some may look at as a non-exotic honeymoon location has become a source of laughter for us now. How could we forget the homeless lady who sat with us for over an hour listening to Sam playing worship music on his guitar?

Without getting into detail, let me just say, during the night of my wedding, I discovered the reason your first time should be with your spouse. It is such a sacred moment, and sharing it with someone you trust and feel safe with makes it even that much more special. It is incredibly beautiful to expose the most vulnerable part of yourself to a person that has made a lifetime commitment before God and man to love and protect you.

I love the verse from Hebrews 13:4 (KJV) that says, *"Marriage is honorable in all, and the bed undefiled."* I was so glad that God had given me the grace to wait, and I was excited about the lifetime of firsts we would have together. That night, I pulled out the first letter I had written to Samuel eight years before knowing who he was, and read it to him. Every word I had written in the letter remained true; when I said, "I do," I meant it with all my heart and meant it for forever.

Chapter 11
Finding Ever After

"I am my beloved's, and his desire is toward me."
~Song of Solomon 7:10

I t was an incredible feeling to wake up every day next to each other, knowing that we were together at last and our married life was finally beginning. Even though we loved being Mr. and Mrs. Okai, we quickly realized day to day living was no fairytale. We had to adjust to a brand new lifestyle as newlyweds and the pressures of house cleaning, cooking, bills, and managing finances quickly started to mount. Sam was adjusting to a new culture, experimenting with new foods, making new friends, and searching for a new job. We were so thankful to have a community at New Life Church in Virginia Beach to help guide us through this new terrain. We had to learn how to become one in our finances, in our recreational life, and in our spiritual life. We discovered each other's quirks and learned how to speak lovingly and patiently to one another. I learned he was straight to the point, and he learned I was an emotional basket case at times.

As the years have progressed, our bond has grown deeper and marriage has become sweeter than the day we first met. I can say with full confidence that I am more in love with Sam today than I was the day of our wedding, because we have never lost sight of the foundation upon which we built our relationship. God has used the triumphs and trials of life to bring us even closer together. Sam always quotes a nugget of truth that we live by, "Marriage is not automatically heaven on earth, you have to put in the work to create heaven on earth." It is so true. We have sown glorious seeds of prayer, love, forgiveness, and understanding in our marriage and watched those seeds bear abundant fruit. God's love and His word have been a rock and a beacon of light for us as our relationship began by faith and continues to this day by faith.

During the early years of marriage, we discovered so many quirks about each other and are still discovering new ones to this day. I learned he likes to crack his knuckles. He discovered my obsession with hand washing and leaving paper towels everywhere. I learned about his undying love for all things soccer— he eats, breathes, and lives the game. If he was not coaching it, he was playing it. If he wasn't playing it, he was watching it. At first, I was tempted to be jealous of the game because it was competing with his time and attention. But then, I remembered the advice I received in premarital counseling to accept each other for who we were. I recognized it was a part of him, it was part of what made him my ice cream man. If I were to love him, I had to love that too. There was even a day I prayed and asked God to give me an understanding and a love for soccer, and over the years, God has truly changed my heart to not only understand it, but even enjoy the game. I support Arsenal, Real Madrid, the Super Eagles of Nigeria; every team my husband loves, I love.

In marriage, we have seen challenges come, but we have also seen the mighty hand of God use those difficulties to bring us even closer together as a unit. We thrive because we know, *"Two are better than one; because they have a good reward for their labor. For if they fall, the one will lift up his fellow: but woe to him that is alone when he falleth; for he hath not another to help him up"* (Ecclesiastes 4:9-10, KJV).

Sam is my best friend, my partner in life, and an amazing father to our children, Emmanuel and Nathaniel. I absolutely adore being married to a beautiful man like him and thank God every day that I get to do life with him by my side. Life itself has not been a fairytale, but being loved and cherished by an incredible man like Samuel has made me feel like I am living my 'ever after' moment like Cinderella. I finally have my prince and the only things left for God to bring our way are a butler, maidservants, and a live-in-nanny.

I can say without a shadow of a doubt, praying and waiting for the right one was so worth it. I found that the practice of self-discipline and abstinence I adhered to during my single years, helped me now that I am married. It helped to build a foundation of commitment and loyalty to my husband that makes my physical, mental, and spiritual connection to him even stronger.

Waiting for the ice cream man taught me about the character of God and enabled me to be able to wait with hope for other promises to manifest in my life. Although it is not always easy, I learned that if you just hang on a little bit longer, you will reap incredible benefits that can only be found by waiting on Him. As the song, *He's Able* by Deitrick Haddon says, "God is able to do what He said He would do, He's going to fulfil every promise to you; don't give up on God, 'cause He won't give up on you, He's able!"

One of the greatest lessons I learned through my journey is that I didn't find love based on my own efforts or strengths. I didn't find love when I wanted to find it. My closest friends and family can attest to the fact that love didn't come to me even when I desperately sought it. I prayed, I fasted, I tried to look pretty, I tried to lose weight and wear the right clothes, I tried to make love work in my own power and in my own strength, but I always hit a brick wall. I ended up feeling hurt, rejected, alone, and sad. I thought love would solve all my problems. I thought love from a guy would fix what was broken in me, I thought it would validate who I was as a woman. I was eager to find love because I hoped it would be my savior.

In the end, I discovered it was Jesus who was my Savior, and He alone brought a sense of purpose and validation that no man could ever fill. I found love because the One who created love heard my prayer and brought my spouse to me in His time. Habakkuk 2:3 (NIV) says, *"For the revelation awaits an appointed time; it speaks of the end and it will not prove false. Though it lingers, wait for it; it will certainly come and will not delay."*

That has been the truth in my life, and I pray it will be the truth in your own life. There is an appointed time for the promises of God to be fulfilled in your life; it is just a matter of receiving the grace to wait for that time to come to pass. When the promise does come, know that whatever it is you are waiting for, as wonderful as it is once it arrives, it will not fulfil you. It will not soothe your deepest hurts or calm all your fears. Only Christ can do that.

As fulfilling as it is to *finally* be with the one I have been waiting for all my life, nothing matches the wonder of knowing God and being in a relationship with Him. God was right all along when He said He would bring someone to walk alongside me in the journey of life, but that person would not be my destination; God has and will forever be my home.

Our First Date

Our Wedding Day

Chapter 12
A Weight Lifted

"I am black, but comely, O ye daughters of Jerusalem,
as the tents of Kedar, as the curtains of Solomon."
~Song of Solomon 1:5

In hindsight, I am so grateful that God was so patient with me throughout my journey of singleness, abstinence, and ultimately marriage. He never mocked me or left me in my weak or naive moments. He would always walk me through, comfort me, affirm me, and tell me that I was beautiful even before I lost forty pounds and became more confident in my own skin.

I recall the season during my teens when my issues with self-image began, and I ate my way through my emotions and insecurities. I didn't feel good about who I saw in the mirror because I kept comparing myself to the girls around me. Most of the girls in my school had fair skin and long straight hair; my skin was dark and my hair thick and coarse. At that time, I had just immigrated with my family from Sydney, Australia to Glastonbury, Connecticut and was overwhelmed by the pressure to make new friends and blend into an American culture that was so unfamiliar to me. I was a Nigerian-Australian immigrant who was searching for identity and struggling to find a voice. My only point of reference to American culture was watching Zach from *Saved By The Bell* date all of the pretty girls at Bayside High, and reading about Jessica Wakefield's latest boyfriend in the *Sweet Valley High* book series. I think that was where I got the false notion that falling in love and having a steady boyfriend would help me to fit in. I assumed having a high school sweetheart would make my transition to a new country a lot smoother. I was wrong.

My transition into a new culture turned out to be anything but smooth. Instead of acceptance, I experienced rejection for the way I looked, talked, and dressed. During my senior year of high school, I called a classmate of mine and asked him out to senior prom, just so I could have someone to go with. He said no. The conversation was so awkward that by the end of it, I was left with a false notion that I wasn't beautiful or worthy of being asked out. I didn't fit into the ideal of beautiful and felt so unwanted that I turned to food for comfort. I recall watching the scale creep up by thirty pounds within just one year. I wanted to get help, but just didn't know how to find it.

When I think back to that time, and compare it to my wedding day, I can't help but be so grateful for how far God has brought me. The day I got married was truly a fulfilment of all the emotions I never thought I would have. I was accepted, loved, and valued just for being me. I got to experience my Cinderella moment with my prince, being completely confident in not only the person I was, but in my own skin.

My encounter with God didn't just change my view of dating, it changed how I saw myself from the inside and out. God taught me to look at myself from

His lens, and from His point of view: I was one of a kind, fearfully, and wonderfully made. After my faith encounter, my relationship with food slowly began to change as my confidence grew, and I began to treat my body as a temple of the Holy Spirit and not a garbage dump. I exercised, ate healthy food portions, and was at peace with my body. The pounds I packed on over the years began to fall off, and by the time I met Sam, I was at my ideal weight. God was even so faithful to help me keep the weight off—even after I had two children. Through my relationship with Christ I learned how to look beyond my imperfections, value myself as a daughter of a King, and embrace the knowledge that He who began a good work in me was faithful to complete it.

Chapter 13
The Ice Cream Man Speaks

"Show me your face, let me hear your voice;
for your voice is sweet,and your face is lovely."
~Song of Songs 2:14

Where do I start from? Meeting my wife, Simisola Okai, was the best thing—after Christ—that has ever happened to me. I remember feeling so humbled the first time I read the letter she had written to me years before she even knew who I was. I thought, WOW! I started reflecting over my life and how I was also looking for love around that same time Simisola had written her letters to me (between 2003 -2007). I was doing everything to please and buy the love of a certain girl I was dating, and she just wouldn't commit. I remember another girl telling me that she didn't love me, and couldn't date or wait for me because of my economic and educational background. But, I am grateful to God that all the wrong places I went searching for love never worked out. After reading the love letter and reflecting on the five years we have spent together as a married couple, I understand better the meaning of true love. I realize that God's plans for us are far better and higher than ours, and I can tell single people reading this book that you don't search love, you wait for love. Prayerfully wait in the right places for love. The love you wait on God for, and find in the right place, will last until death do you part; but the one you search and settle for, can cause you great pain and heartbreak.

I had been in about three serious relationships prior to meeting Simisola that I tried to use my human power to make work. They all fell apart, leaving me broken and feeling like maybe marriage was not meant for me. Now, I really understand better Proverbs 19:21

(KJV) that says, *"There are many devices in a man's heart; nevertheless the counsel of the Lord, that shall stand."*

I recall our first meeting and knowing in my heart that it was orchestrated by God. The first time I laid eyes on Simisola, was at Realm of Glory Church in Abuja, Nigeria, as I was leading praise and worship. The song I was singing that day was "How Great is Our God." What first attracted me to her was seeing her lost in worship, and I remember saying to myself on stage, *that is my wife.*

Prior to that time, I had always prayed for a woman that loved the presence of God, not just the presents (gifts) from Him, and a woman who feared God and had the capacity for everything it took to be a wife. On our first date, I was battling with how I should behave in front of Simisola. I decided I was not going to try and impress her, rather I would just be myself. When we went to the cafe at Ceddi Plaza, I remember not having a lot of money on me and praying that she would eat the cheapest food on the menu. When it was time to make an order, I asked her to pick whatever she wanted, and she said no, she was fine with whatever I picked. I told her to just pick anything and I would pay, but she kept insisting that I pick something. As I looked at the expensive menu, something in me kept telling me *keep it simple, be yourself, and don't try to impress her.*

I wanted to let her see my true level and take me for who I was and not just what I had. When I say true level (economic, spiritual, and physical state), I knew I didn't want to fake who I was in waiting and looking for love. I didn't want a situation where I put myself under unnecessary pressure and stress. I was told by my mentors that I would endure and not enjoy marriage if I wasn't true to myself. A person who loves you for who you are will stay and be there for you in all seasons of life, be it good or bad, sickness, pain, rain or sunshine. People who love you only for what you have will not be there for you when it matters. They are not faithful, committed, or trustworthy. They are not consistent in their ways, and will leave you when you need them the most.

All relationships have high and low moments, and you need a good hearted and loving person to do life with; that is what I have in my wife, Simisola Okai. We are not perfect, nor do we come from perfect families, but the love we have for each other is bigger than our faults and imperfections. I can say without hesitation that I am glad I never settled while looking and waiting for love, because God gave me the best when the time was right.

I am glad that I bought Simisola ice cream that day and glad that my pride did not get in the way and push me to take her somewhere that was above my level. The interesting part was that, after I bought the ice cream, the reaction on her face kind of scared me. I remember her looking surprised and sober, and thinking, *I have messed up this opportunity to have a good woman.* But later on, I discovered that wasn't the case, and she had prayed a long time ago that God would tell the man that she would marry to take her out for her ice cream on their first date. I had no clue about that prayer until after I told her about my intentions to spend the rest of my life with her. In the end, everything worked out well; we both had a peace about being together and everyone around us could see God was the center of our relationship.

If I could give any advice to singles today, it would be, "The right person is worth waiting for." I know waiting isn't easy, because I have been there and felt lonely, depressed, and heart broken. I have given love and gotten pain and rejection back. I had emotional pain, I felt ugly and unattractive, and even wondered if maybe God had forgotten me. The wait was hard because I wasn't sure if my desire would ever come to pass.

The truth is, it takes waiting to hear from God. It takes prayerfully watching to see what God is doing; it takes moving by faith to experience, or to bring to manifestation, the things He desires for you. The Bible says in James 2:17 (KJV), *"Even so faith, if it hath not works, is dead."* Many singles are waiting, but they are not watching and taking steps of faith to bring to manifestation what God has already prepared for them. It is very important that, while single—while waiting— we watch so that what God has prepared doesn't elude us.

The Bible says it will be done unto you according to your faith. Keep the faith that God has a person out there for you and remember the verse from Jeremiah 29:11(KJV) that says, *"For I know the thoughts I think towards you, saith the LORD, thoughts of peace, and not of evil, to give you an expected end."* Know that God wants better for you than you even want for yourself. Trust Him, because He is the One that has placed the desire for a loving partner there.

The time of waiting is not always easy. There may be times when you will be lonely or depressed. There may even be times when you meet who you think is "the one" only to discover he or she is a counterfeit. Don't settle while waiting. People who settle after waiting always end up enduring marriage instead of enjoying it. Marriage is meant to be enjoyed and not just tolerated.

Proverbs 10:22 (KJV) says, " *The blessing of the LORD, it maketh rich, and he addeth no sorrow with it.*" Marriage is for life, and not for a moment. So why settle and go through the frustration and pain of being with the wrong person? If you wait for the fullness of God's appointed time and person, you will enjoy marriage for the rest of your life. Even if it takes waiting in the rain or storm, being rejected and mocked, or enduring loneliness—wait. The right person and the will of God is worth waiting for.

During your season of singleness, I would also say learn to actively wait. Your single years are a vital time to build your relationship with God through prayer and studying the Bible. Jeremiah 33:3(KJV) says, *"Call to me, and I will answer thee, and show thee great and mighty things, which thou knowest not."* Today, I am married to the love of my life. I have never been so happy and fulfilled like I have been since I met my wife. She has made me a better person. I will choose her over and over again because she completes me.

~Sam Okai, a.k.a The Ice Cream Man

Chapter 14
It's Not About The Ice Cream

*"Many waters cannot quench love, neither can the
floods drown it."*
~ Song of Solomon 8:7

I have shared my story with several people over the
years and oftentimes I have heard people say, "I am
waiting for my ice cream man," or "I need to go
to the ice cream store and order me a vanilla cone," or
something along those lines. Some girlfriends have even
said, "It sounds so easy for you Simi, you pray and God

sends you your perfect guy. I pray, and wait for years and either nobody shows up or I get Bobo the Clown." I laugh when they make comments like that, yet inside my heart I am thinking, "It's not about the ice cream!" It really isn't about the ice cream.

This book isn't a how-to guide showing you the ten easy steps to find your ice cream man. The reason I am sharing my story is so you can know that God is indeed the author of romance, and He wants to develop a language with you so you can also know when He has led you to the person that will walk alongside you as your life partner. God wants you to know that He cares about helping you not only to connect with the right person, but also to develop your character so that when He does join you together, you will be a blessing and not a burden to each other. Ice cream just happened to be the language that God used to communicate to me and confirm who my husband would be. The ice cream was my Gideon's fleece with God. Yet, I know, God can use anything to speak to you; you just need to be open to receive it.

I think the story of David and Goliath serves as a perfect example. When David defeated Goliath, he used a weapon that was familiar to him and conquered a giant with just a sling and a stone. A sling and a stone was not a tool that people normally went into battle with. When most people think of entering a fight, they imagine wearing full armor and carrying an assault weapon—like a heavy sword or a rifle. Despite these truths, David entered the battle with just a sling and a stone. It was with these unlikely weapons that he was able to defeat Goliath. The significance was not in the object David used, but in David's relationship with God. That was what ultimately led David to experience victory.

The tool that helped me discern God's perfect will for my marriage happened to be ice cream—not because there is something special about ice cream, but because God knew that was something I enjoyed. In David's story, he was familiar with the sling and a stone. He had plenty of experience training with it. In fact, Saul attempted to convince David to wear his armor because it was what "everybody else did." It was how battles were won. However, because David had a relationship with God, He had confidence in using a tool God had already given him.

The "Sauls" of this world will try to tell you that you

need to sleep around in order to find your spouse. The world will tell you that you need to date as many people as possible, experiment sexually with them, and base your choice solely upon how attracted you are to them. The God of David would tell you otherwise. The God that was faithful to lead me to my husband is faithful to lead you to your spouse. All you have to do is trust Him. My testimony is that you don't have to go through a million heartbreaks just to experience lasting love. I was a virgin when I got married and my husband was my first serious relationship and the true love of my life. Your story doesn't have to look like mine. Maybe your past relationships have been negative ones, or maybe you didn't wait until marriage to have sex. Whatever your case may be, know that it's never too late to start over. God is a God of second chances and will never condemn you for your past mistakes.

God said in 2 Corinthians 6:2 (NIV), *"Now is the accepted time; behold, now is the day of salvation."* Today is the day you can start over and watch God move in incredible ways on your behalf. My prayer is that you will get to know God for yourself and have confidence in the life tools He has already given you, so that you will hear God clearly when He is leading you to your life partner. You can use my ice cream story as your inspiration, but know God is not limited in the tools He can use to lead you to your promise. The sling and stones were David's tool; ice cream was mine. You can develop your own language with the One who created you, all you need to do is ask Him in faith.

Prayer

Heavenly Father,
I pray for those who are reading this book today
looking for love, for those who have given up on love,
for the heartbroken, and for mothers and fathers who
desire godly spouses for their children. I pray that You
would grant them their hearts' desires just like You
did for me. Holy Spirit do exceedingly, abundantly,
above and beyond anything they could ask or
imagine, and help them to see that You are indeed the
author of romance.
In Jesus name I pray,
Amen

Epilogue
Waiting in Style

Waiting. Nobody likes the idea. It seems as though we are always waiting for something. We wait impatiently for our food to arrive at a restaurant. We wait for our favorite show to come on television, or we wait for the sun to rise the next morning. Old or young, we are all waiting for something—some in eager expectation, some in despondency and despair.

If we must wait, why not do it in style? Wait in a posture of expectation. Wait with a smile on your face. Wait in a manner that anyone looking at you would never guess you were waiting. Wait with hope. As you wait, ask yourself, "What is my posture?" Are you waiting in hope and excitement with your arms wide open? Or are you presenting a posture of complete misery, so desperate to get past the waiting period that everything around you turns completely sour.

Understand that if it is God you are waiting for, you are on His clock, not your own. Remember what the Bible says about God's time: "One day is with the Lord as a thousand years, and a thousand years as one day" (2 Peter 3:8, KJV). Waiting in faith requires us to take the focus off self and place it on God. A wise prophet Isaiah once said, "But they that wait upon the Lord shall renew their strength; they shall mount up with wings as eagles; they shall run, and not be weary; and they shall walk, and not faint" (Isaiah 40:31, KJV).

Interestingly enough, to "wait on" something or someone is not to remain inactive or passive. It means "to perform the duties of an attendant or servant," to "supply the wants of a person, as serving a meal," or "to call upon or visit." In waiting on God, we are performing an intimate, deliberate, purposeful act of service and worship. In doing so, God renews our strength and transforms the lull and hum-drum of waiting, into something fresh and exciting as we behold His glory.

Waiting can be transformed from something we dread, into something beautiful, especially when we know the purpose for the wait. For example, you decide to bake a special cake for your guests during Sunday dinner. When you bake the cake, you place the batter in the oven and wait. Why? Because you understand that if you take it out five minutes after you place it in the oven, it would not be ready. You have an expected end that in twenty-five minutes, your cake will be done. Within the twenty-five minutes, you could stare hopelessly at the oven, frustrated that the cake is not ready to be eaten. Or you could spend the twenty-five minutes entertaining your guests, playing a game of scrabble, and laughing so hard you forget all about the cake until you hear the oven timer beeping. The lesson comes in making the best use of the time you spend waiting. Productivity during the waiting period allows you to build character, and brings you to your final destination in style. Once you know the purpose of the wait, the ride becomes a lot smoother and much more purposeful.

They say the best way to change old habits is to replace them with new ones; instead of waiting impatiently, wait with style. So, to all of you holding out, don't lose hope. You can rest assured that when it is "God's time, it's God's dime." With God's timing, there is always provision. Take the advice of a young youth pastor: "God's clock is never easy to watch, so don't."

So that young, attractive, smart, AND funny millionaire of a spouse you are waiting for? They're out there. That promotion you have been waiting on as you faithfully clock in fifty plus hours a week; it's on its way. While you wait, why not start a small business of your own? Who knows, you might discover the next billion-dollar chip and meet your spouse in the process.

As you stand waiting for that next level—for the reconciliation of a relationship, for a future spouse, or simply for the next bus to arrive—remember God's promise from Isaiah 49:23(KJV), "I am the Lord: for they shall not be ashamed that wait for me."

Believe me when I say that you are just one ice cream cone away from receiving your promise.

Share Your Thoughts With The Author :

Write to SamSimStream@gmail.com

CPSIA information can be obtained
at www.ICGtesting.com
Printed in the USA
BVOW11s1631100817
491571BV00016B/157/P

9 781945 304811